Disney Numbers & Counting

Table of Contents

**Number Concepts:
Same, More, and Fewer**

The Same Game 2
Give Me More! 3
Count and Color 4

**Recognizing and Writing
Numbers 1 Through 5**

Buzz Is Number 1 5
2 at a Time 6
Do You See 3? 7
4 in a Row 8
5 Fun Foods 9

**Ordinals
First Through Fifth**

Today's Talent Show 10

**Recognizing and Writing
Numbers 6 Through 10**

Pick 6 11
7 Silly Hats 12
Wait for 8 13
9 Is Nice 14
10 Is Tricky 15

**Ordinals
Sixth Through Tenth**

Let's Visit Bambi 16

**Reviewing Ordinals
First Through Tenth**

Follow the Path 17

**Reviewing Numbers
1 Through 10**

How Many Bones? 18

**Recognizing and Writing Numbers
11 Through 20**

Lots of Spots (11, 12) 19
Sunflower Fun (13, 14) 20
Money in the Bank (15, 16) 21
Bright Lights for Lumiere (17, 18) 22
Help Simba and Nala Count (19, 20) ... 23

**Reviewing Numbers
11 Through 20**

Counting With Pooh 24, 25

**Reviewing Numbers
1 Through 20**

Come Sail Away 26, 27
Circus Time 28, 29

Helping Your Child at Home 30
Answer Key 31, 32

Copyright © Disney Enterprises, Inc. All rights reserved. Pixar propertis ©Disney/Pixar.
Based on the "Winnie the Pooh" works, by A.A. Milne and E.H. Shepard

Number Concept: Same

The Same Game

Help Ariel and Flounder. Match a big sea horse with a little sea horse that is the same color.

Name

Count the little sea horses. Count the big sea horses. Is the number of each the **same**?

© Disney/Pixar

Number Concept: More

Name

Give Me More!

Sebastian has **more** pink shells than blue shells. Now look at the other plants. Circle the plant in each box that has **more** fish swimming through it.

© Disney/Pixar

Number Concept: Fewer

Count and Color

Fewer means less. Help Rex decide which toy has **fewer** stars, spots, and dots.

Color the toy with fewer stars.

a. 　　b.

Color the toy with fewer spots.

c. 　　d.

Color the toy with fewer dots.

e. 　　f.

© Disney/Pixar

Recognizing and Writing 1

Buzz Is Number 1

Name

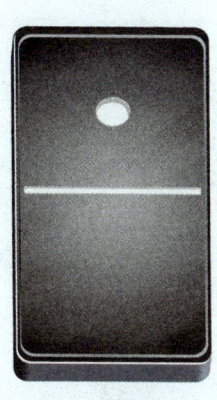

1

Circle the pictures that show 1.
Then, trace and write the number **1**.

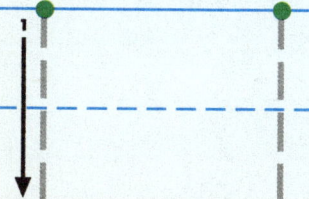

5

© Disney/Pixar

Recognizing and Writing 2

2 at a Time

Name

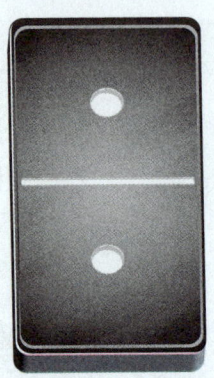

Can you find 2 Dalmatians? Circle each group of 2. Then, trace and write the number **2**.

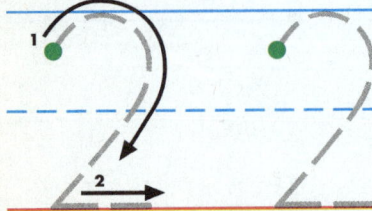

Based on the book
The Hundred and One Dalmatians by
Dodie Smith, published by The Viking Press.

© Disney/Pixar

Recognizing and Writing 3

Do You See 3?

Name

3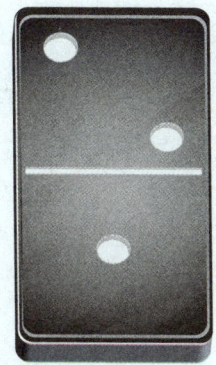

Help Mater count the tires. Circle each group of 3. Then, trace and write the number **3**.

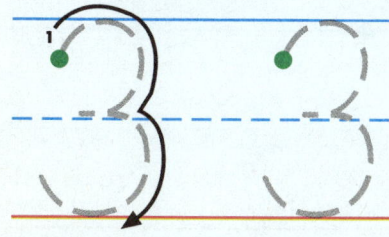

Recognizing and Writing 4

4 in a Row

Name

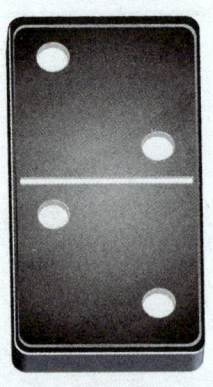

Help Timon and Pumbaa count their friends' footprints. Count and circle 4 footprints in each row. Then, trace and write the number **4**.

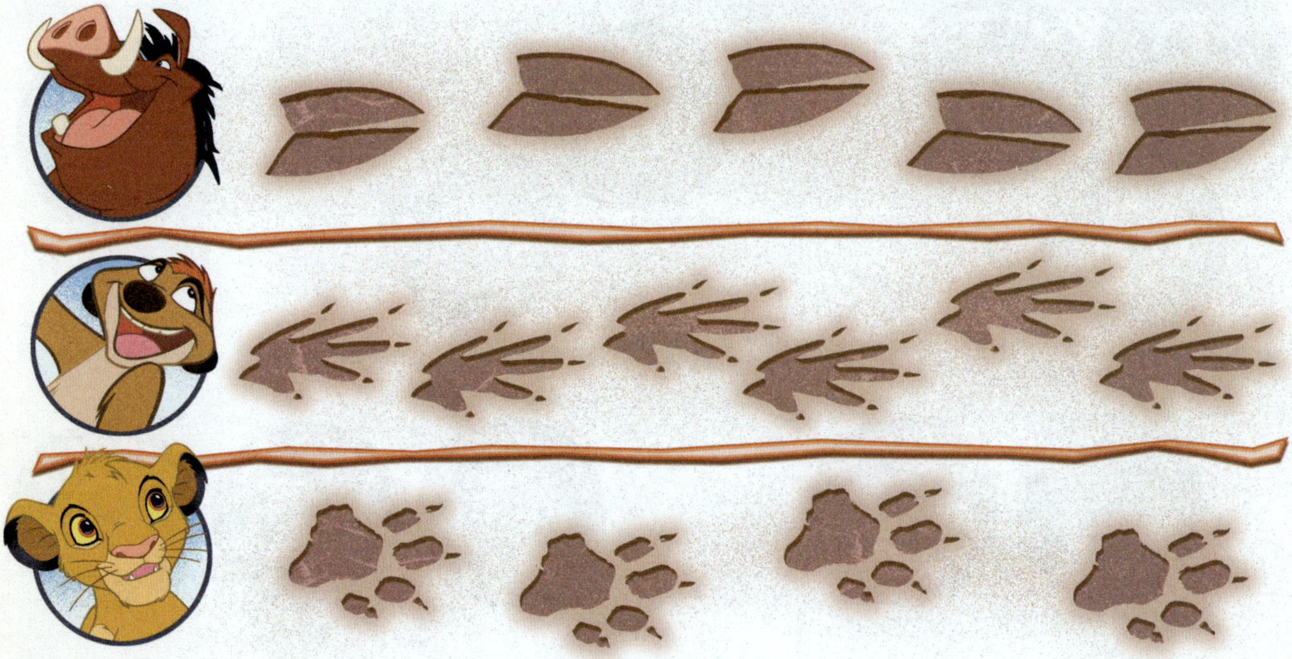

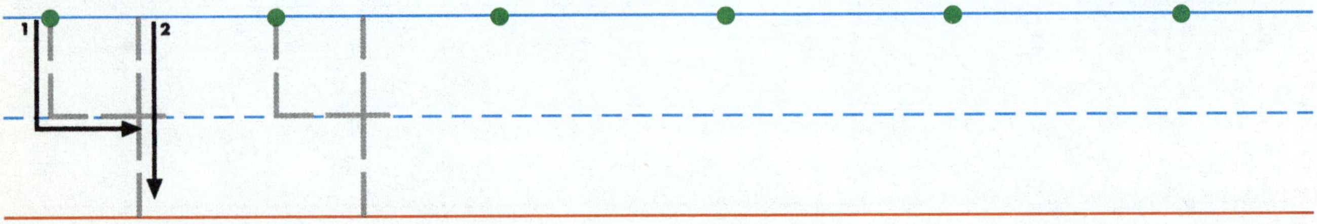

Recognizing and Writing 5

5 Fun Foods

Name

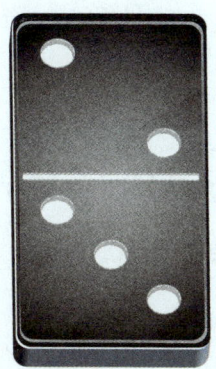

Heimlich loves the circus! What can you see and do at a circus? First, circle 5 foods. Then, trace and write the number **5**.

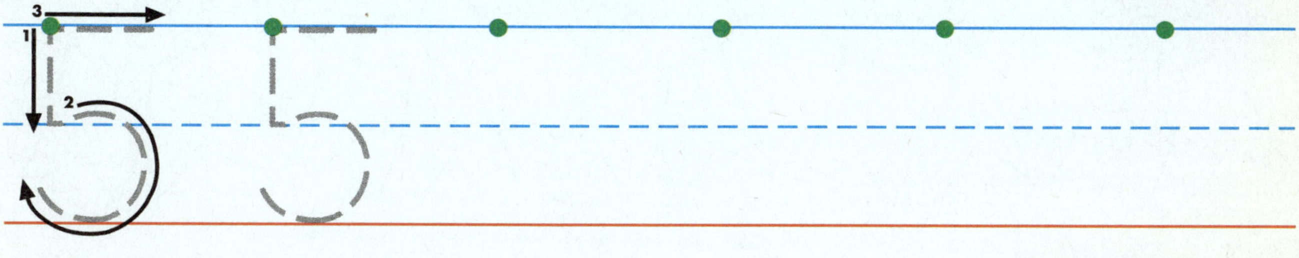

© Disney/Pixar

Ordinals First Through Fifth

Today's Talent Show

Name

Pooh and his friends are having a talent show. They will all win a ribbon. Follow the directions below.

Color the **third** ribbon ⬛ (yellow)   Color the **fourth** ribbon ⬛ (green)

Color the **fifth** ribbon ⬛ (orange)   Color the **second** ribbon ⬛ (red)

Color the **first** ribbon ⬛ (blue)

© Disney/Pixar

Based on the "Winnie the Pooh" works by A.A. Mine and E.H. Shepard.

Recognizing and Writing 6

Pick 6

Name

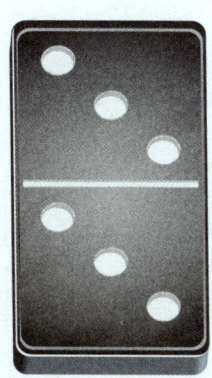

Pooh will show Piglet how to make a kite. There are 6 circles on Pooh's kite. Color each kite that has 6 shapes on it. Then, trace and write the number **6**.

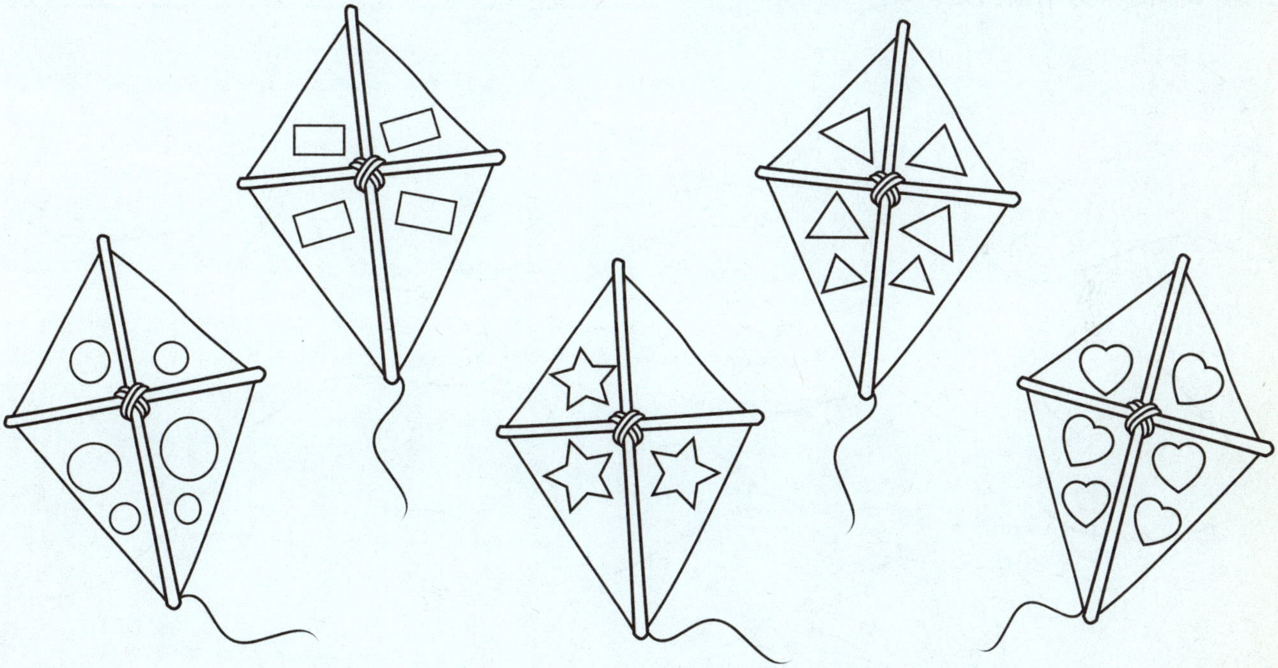

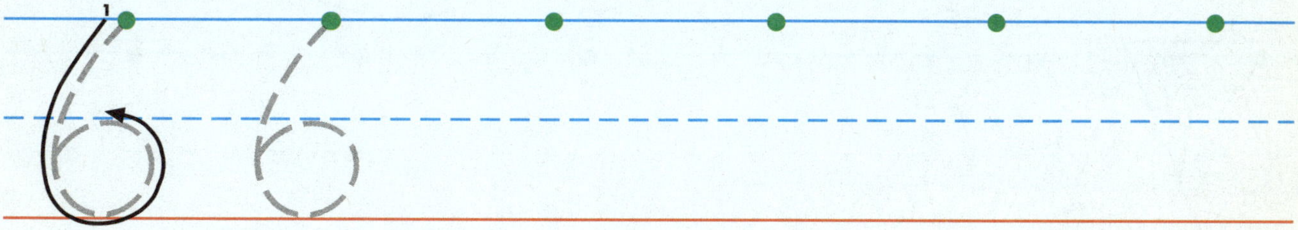

Based on the "Winnie the Pooh" works by A.A. Mine and E.H. Shepard.

© Disney/Pixar

Recognizing and Writing 7

Name

7 Silly Hats

7

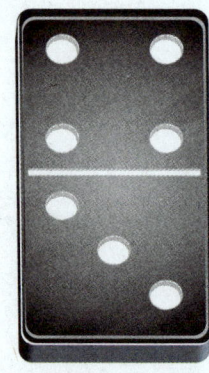

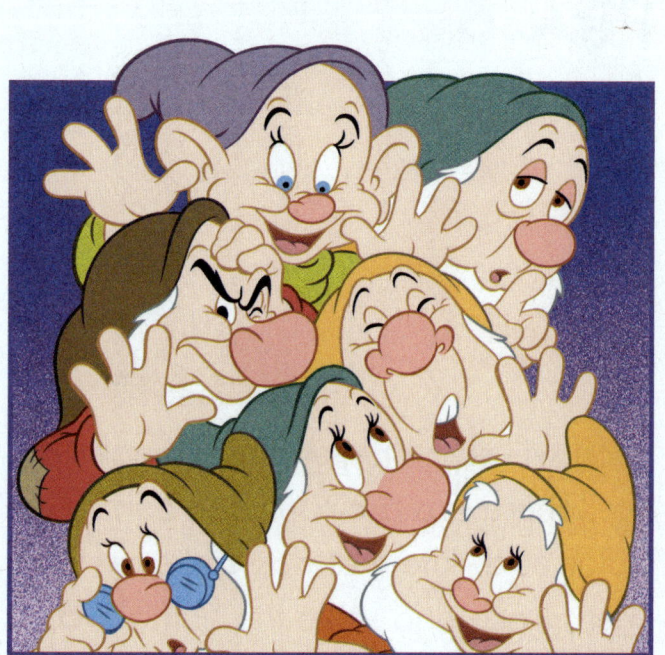

Can you count how many Dwarfs there are? Of course, there are 7. Count and color 7 hats. Then, trace and write the number **7**.

1

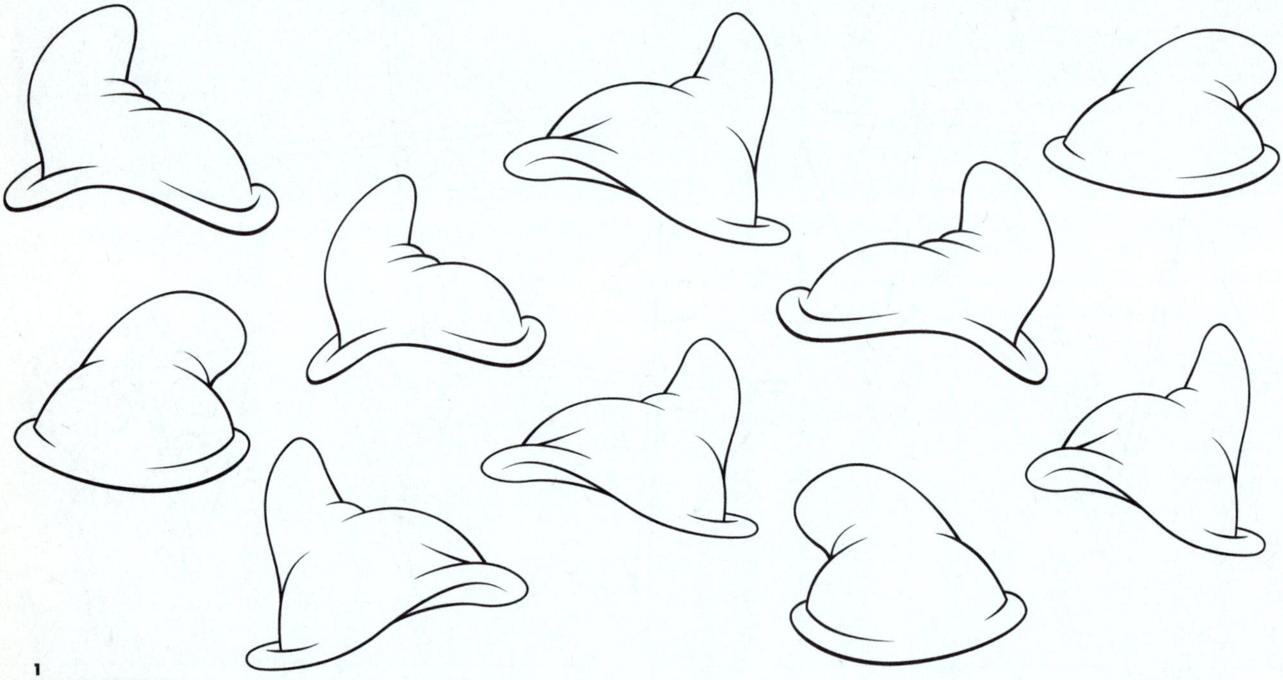

Recognizing and Writing 8

Wait for 8

Name _____

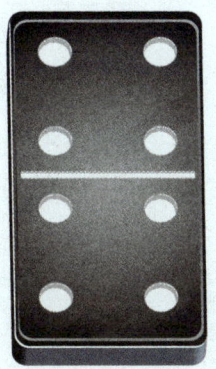

Lightning loves to see the checkered flag at the finish line. Count how many flags you see below. Then, trace and write the number **8**.

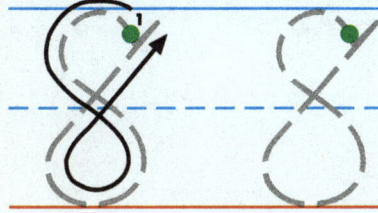

Recognizing and Writing 9

9 Is Nice

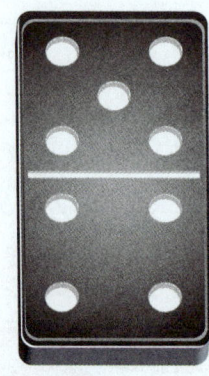

Name _____

Count the things in each group. Draw a line from each group that has 9 things to the number 9. Then, trace and write the number 9.

© Disney/Pixar

Recognizing and Writing 10

10 Is Tricky

10

Try a trick like Manny does. Draw 10 legs on the bug. Then, make it turn a different color. **Hint:** Your crayons will help you do this trick! Then, trace and write the number **10**.

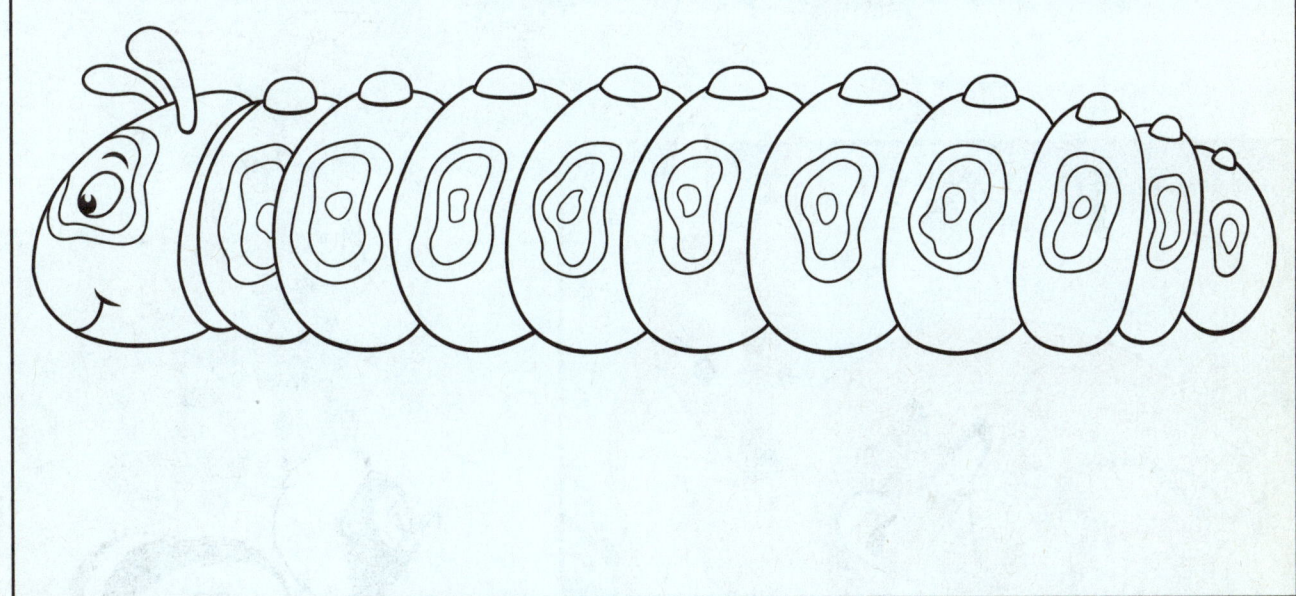

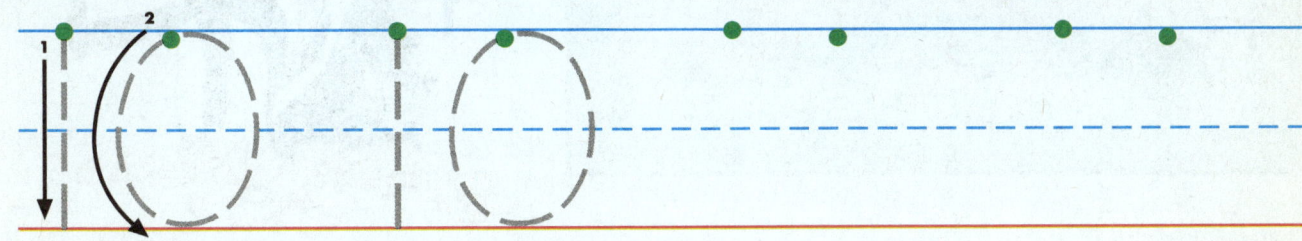

Ordinals Sixth Through Tenth

Let's Visit Bambi

Name _____

Ten animals are waiting to visit Bambi. Beginning with Flower, point to the **sixth**, **seventh**, **eighth**, **ninth**, and **tenth** animal in line. Then, follow the directions below.

Start with Flower. Circle the **sixth** animal.
Draw a box around the **eighth** animal.
Draw an **X** on the **tenth** animal.

Reviewing Ordinals First Through Tenth

Name _____

Follow the Path

Help Aladdin get to Princess Jasmine along the path of lamps. Follow the directions below.

Color the **first** lamp 🟩.   Color the **seventh** lamp 🟦.

Color the **fourth** lamp 🟧.   Color the **tenth** lamp 🟨.

© Disney/Pixar

Reviewing Numbers 1 Through 10

How Many Bones?

Name _____

Count and write how many bones you see in each box. Then, fill in the missing numbers from **1** to **10**.

a.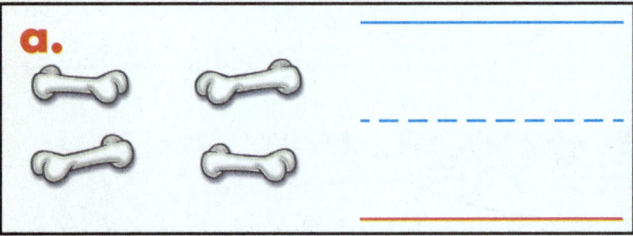

b.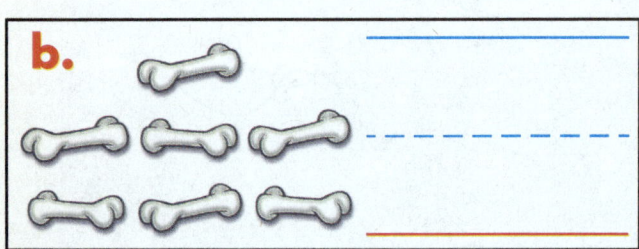

d.

c.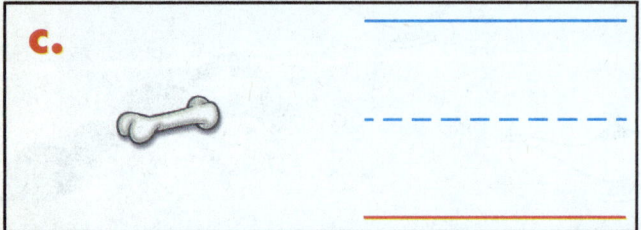

e.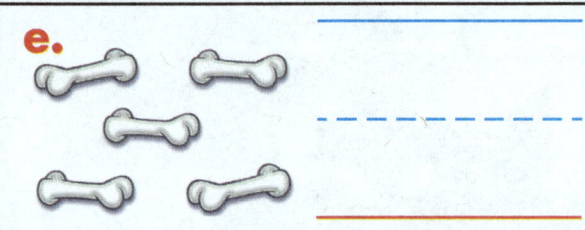

1 ___ 3 ___ 5

___ 7 ___ 9 ___

Recognizing and Writing 11 and 12

Name _____

Lots of Spots

Draw 11 spots on the first puppy and 12 spots on the second puppy. Then, trace and write the numbers **11** and **12**.

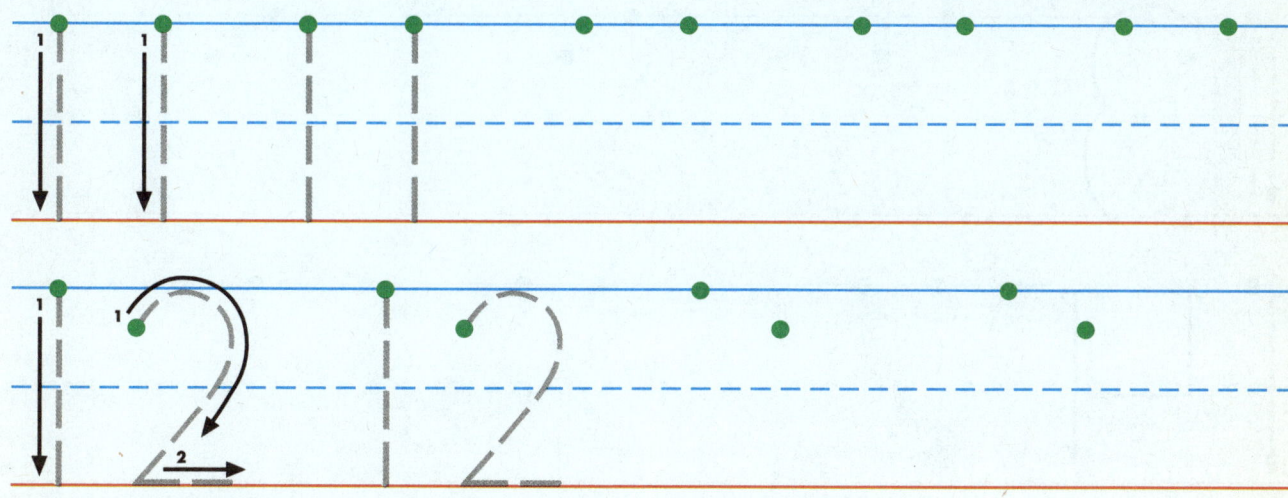

Based on the book
The Hundred and One Dalmatians by
Dodie Smith, published by The Viking Press.

Recognizing and Writing 13 and 14

Sunflower Fun

Pocahontas is picking sunflowers. Follow the directions below. Then, trace and write the numbers **13** and **14**.

a. How many sunflowers are there? _____

b. Color 13 sunflowers.

Recognizing and Writing 15 and 16

Money in the Bank

Name _____

Help Andy count. Follow the directions below. Then, trace and write the numbers **15** and **16**.

a. How many pennies are there? _____

b. Andy wants to put 15 cents in his piggy bank. Color 15 pennies.

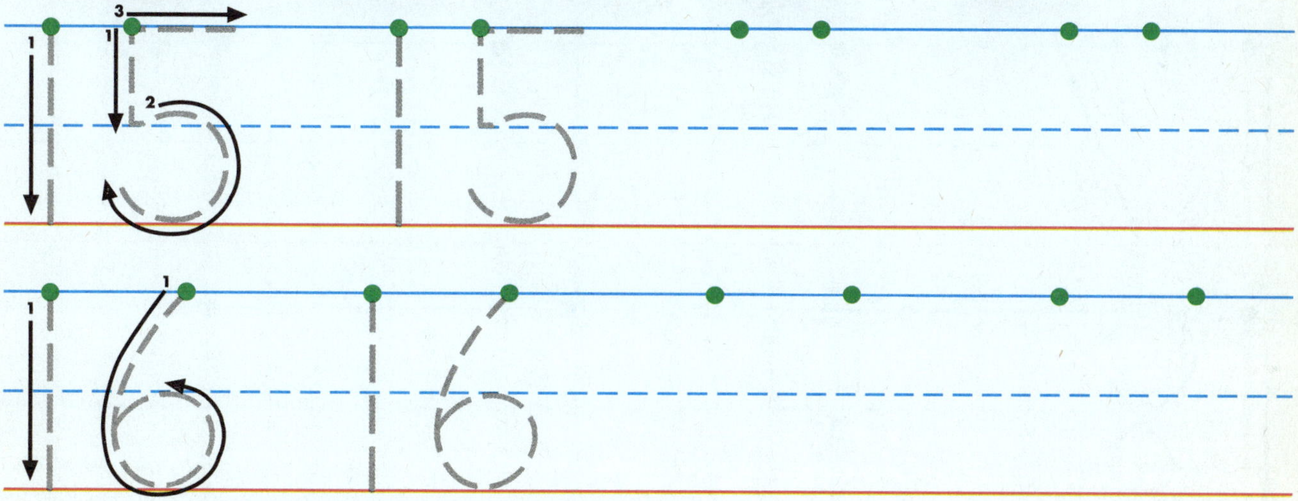

15 15

16 16

21

© Disney/Pixar

Recognizing and Writing 17 and 18

Bright Lights for Lumiere

Follow the directions below. Then, trace and write the numbers **17** and **18**.

a. How many candles are there?

b. How many candles are green?

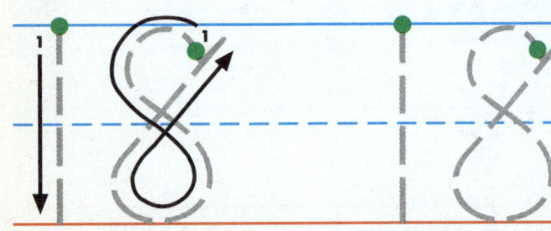

Recognizing and Writing 19 and 20

Name

Counting Bugs

Count how many of each bug you see. Write the correct number. Then, trace and write the numbers **19** and **20**.

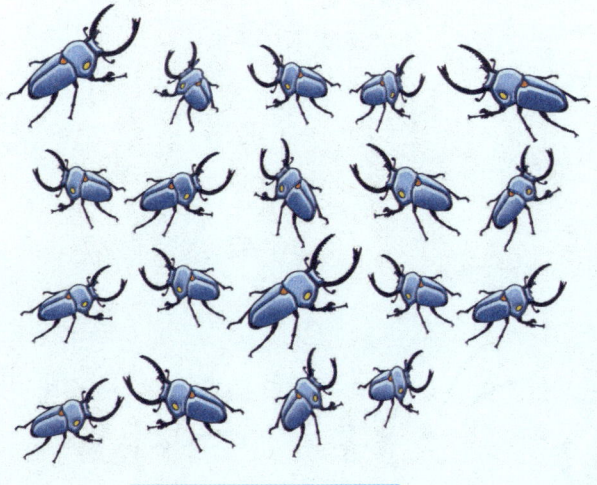

a.

b.

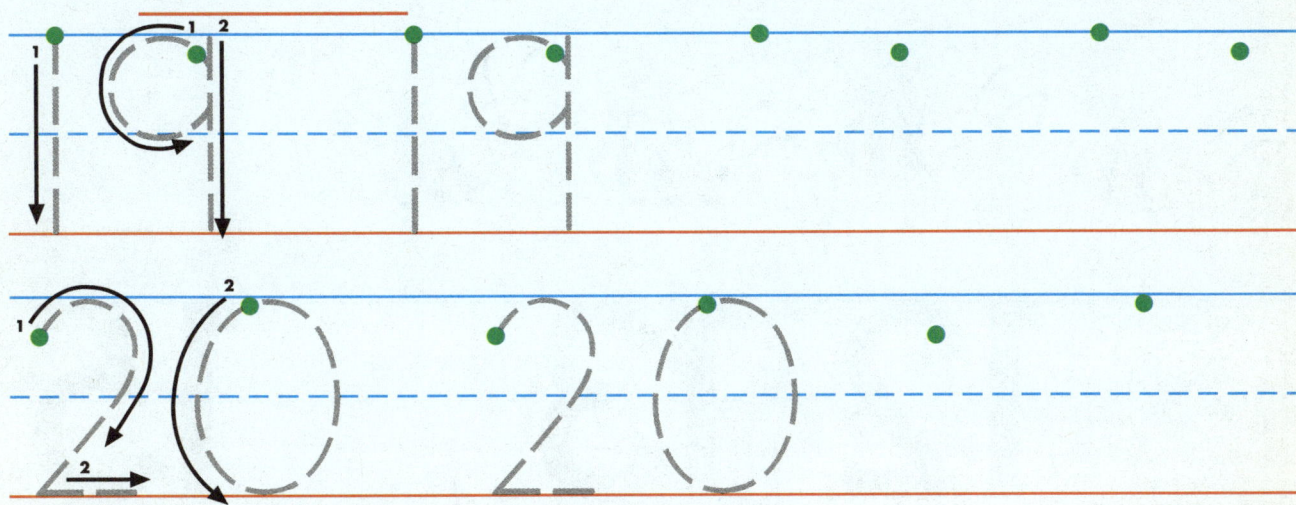

Reviewing Numbers 11 Through 20

Name _____

Counting with Pooh

Help Pooh and Piglet count all the bees, flowers, and butterflies. On each line, write how many of each you see. Then, count from **11** to **20** by filling in the missing numbers below.

a. _____

12   13   ___   15

Reviewing Numbers 11 Through 20

Name _____

b. _____

c. _____

16   18 19 20

Reviewing Numbers 1 Through 20

Come Sail Away

Name

Count from **1** to **20** by filling in the missing numbers. Then, connect the dots on the next page in order from **1** to **20** around Ariel and Prince Eric. Color the picture.

1   3   5

7   9

11   13   15

17   19

© Disney/Pixar

Reviewing Numbers 1 Through 20

Name

27

Reviewing Numbers 1 Through 20

Name

Circus Time

You will need:
- one die (or a spinner or six cards numbered 1–6)
- a different marker for each player

Number of players: 2–4

How to play: Give each player a different marker. Put all of the markers on the space that says **START**. Take turns rolling the die. Each player counts and moves the number of spaces shown on the die. If a player lands on a bug, he or she stays on that space. If a player lands on another space, he or she follows what it says to do. The object of the game is to reach the **FINISH** space first.

© Disney/Pixar

Reviewing Numbers 1 Through 20

Name

Letter to the Parent

Helping Your Child at Home
Name

Numbers and Counting

Children see numbers all around them—at the grocery store, on the front of houses, in books, and on the telephone. Helping your child learn how to recognize, write, and begin to understand numbers are all very important math concepts. Learning how to count is also a skill that should be learned early on. Start with teaching your child how to count up to 5, then to 10, and eventually up to 20. The activities in this workbook and those suggested below are practical ways you can help your child learn all about numbers and get him or her counting in no time. Remember to have fun working and learning together with your child!

- Before or after bathtime have your child count his or her fingers and toes.

- Teach your child the numbers in your phone number and address.

- Have your child read numbers on signs when you go to the grocery store.

- Help your child practice typing the numbers 1–20 on the computer. Then print out the numbers and have your child practice reading them.

- Show your child cards from a deck of playing cards. Have him or her count the hearts, clubs, spades, or diamonds on each card.

© Disney/Pixar

Answer Key

Name

Page 2

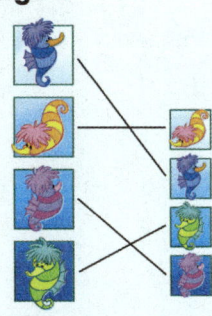

Answer: YES

Page 3

Page 4

Color b, c, and f.

Page 5

Page 6

Page 7

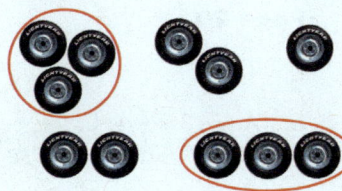

Page 8

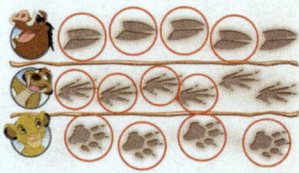

Page 9
Any 5 pictures may be circled.

Page 10

Page 11

Page 12
Any 7 hats may be colored.

Page 14

Page 15

© Disney/Pixar

Answer Key

Name

Page 16

Page 17

Page 18

a. 4
b. 7
c. 1
d. 3
e. 5

Page 19

Page 20

a. 14
b. Any 13 flowers may be colored.

Page 21

a. 16
b. Any 15 pennies may be colored.

Page 22

a. 18
b. 17

Page 23

a. 19
b. 20

Pages 24 and 25

a. 17
b. 14
c. 11

Page 27

32

© Disney/Pixar